LET'S VISIT JAPAN

Let's visit
JAPAN

JOHN C. CALDWELL

BURKE

First published in Great Britain July 1965
Reprinted November 1966
Second revised edition April 1969
Third revised edition June 1974
Fourth revised edition January 1980
Fifth revised edition 1984
© John C. Caldwell 1959
New material included in this edition © Burke Publishing Company Limited 1965, 1969, 1974, 1980 and 1984.

CIP data
Caldwell, John C. (John Cope)
    Let's visit Japan – 5th ed.
    1. Japan – Social life and customs – Juvenile literature
    I. Title
    952.04   DS822.5
    ISBN 0 222 01028 2

Burke Publishing Company Limited
Pegasus House, 116–120 Golden Lane,EC1Y 0TL, England.
Burke Publishing (Canada) Limited
Registered Office: 20 Queen Street West, Suite 3000, Box 30, Toronto, Canada M5H 1V5.
Burke Publishing Company Inc.
Registered Office: 333 State Street, PO Box 1740, Bridgeport, Connecticut 06601, U.S.A.
Filmset in "Monophoto" Baskerville by Green Gates Studios Ltd., Hull, England.
Printed in Singapore by Tien Wah Press (Pte.) Ltd.

Contents

ACKNOWLEDGEMENTS

The Publishers are grateful to the Press Section of the Embassy of Japan and to L. A. Bester for assistance in the preparation of this edition, and to the Japan Tourist Office for permission to reproduce the photograph of Hirosaki Castle which appears on the cover of this book. The majority of the photographs in the book were taken by the Author. Others were supplied by R. Estall, Ray Halin, J.P.I., The International Society for Educational Information, The Japan Travel Bureau, Monitor Press Features, Ian Mutsu and the United States Air Force.

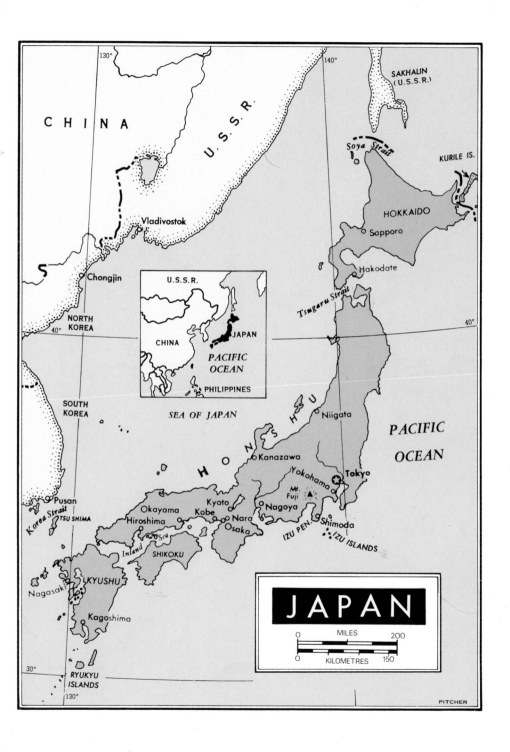

Let's Visit Japan

Can you name things for which Japan and its people are famous?

Japan is known all over the world for its beautiful temples and shrines. Japanese cherry trees are famous, and hundreds of these trees have been planted in Europe. Japan is also famous for one of the world's most beautiful mountains. Mt. Fuji is a dormant volcano, and its snow-capped cone is very frequently photographed.

Can you think of a Japanese word that is often used in our country? The word *kimono* has become a part of our language. The kimono is a loose-fitting garment like a dressing gown, held in place by a closely-wound wide sash.

There are many reasons why we should know more about this country, its past, present and future. Japan is the greatest industrial nation in Asia. This means that Japan has many factories which make everything from watches to huge ocean-going ships. The Japanese are good businessmen, and our countries trade with each other. This means that the Japanese factories make many things which we buy.

9

So there we have a few of the reasons why Japan is important to us. It is a nation of factories, and its people are the best businessmen in Asia.

In this book we shall learn more about Japan and its people. We shall read about its history and how the Japanese live. But perhaps the best way to begin our visit to Japan is to learn about its geography.

Mt. Fuji, Japan's most famous mountain

Mt. Aso on Kyushu, the largest active volcano in the world

A Land of Islands and Mountains

Let's look at the map and see just where Japan is located. You will see that the country is made up of many islands which lie next to the eastern coasts of China and Korea.

11

The islands of Japan stretch for over 2,400 kilometres (1,500 miles) from north to south.

This means that the climate of Japan is much like that of America. In the north the winters are very cold. In the far south it is much warmer. Around Tokyo, Japan's capital city, the weather is much like that of Washington, the American capital. There is some snow in the winter, and it is damp and cold. Summers can be quite hot and sticky.

Japan is made up of islands and mountains. Hokkaido and Kyushu are the big islands at the northern and southern ends of the long chain of Japanese islands. Honshu is the "middle" island, and by far the largest. To the south of Honshu is Shikoku which is the smallest of the four big islands. Kyushu is to the south of Shikoku. In between and all along the coasts of these four big islands are hundreds of others. Some are large enough to have villages on them. Others are merely tiny rocks.

Everywhere, from the far north to the tip of Kyushu, there are mountains. These mountains are volcanic, which means that there is eruptive activity beneath the earth's surface. When there is an eruption, lava—or hot molten rock— bursts up through the mountain top and lava pours down its sides. We might say that all the land beneath Japan is on fire. Mt. Fuji, the most famous peak, is a dormant volcano. This means that steam, smoke and lava no longer pour from its crater. But there are other mountains which are still active volcanoes.

This volcanic activity underneath the soil of Japan produces

Much of Japan's coast is rocky and barren like this

thousands of hot springs. There are places where steam and hot water pour from the ground. There is one city in Japan where there are seven hundred hot springs. There are several places which the Japanese call "hells", where hundreds of these geysers gush out.

All this activity underneath Japan produces something else: earthquakes. Sometimes the earthquakes cause a great deal of damage. The last bad one was in 1923. At that time, nearly 100,000 Japanese lost their lives; both Tokyo and the great city of Yokohama were seriously affected.

13

Although the Japanese islands stretch over 2,400 kilometres (1,500 miles) from north to south, the total land area of Japan is only about 370,000 square kilometres (142,812 square miles). This means that, comparing it to other countries in Asia, Japan is somewhat larger in area than the Philippines or Vietnam. But while the population of the Philippines is about 50 million the population of Japan is about 118 million.

We can realize at once that Japan is a very crowded country. It is not one of the large countries in area, but it is the seventh most populous in the world. Since there are mountains everywhere, and many of these are too steep even for small villages, the few flat places in Japan are terribly crowded. It is a land of big cities. Tokyo, with a population of nearly twelve million, is one of the world's largest metropolitan centres. It is located on the big island of Honshu, on a flat area called the Kanto Plain.

As we shall learn, one of Japan's great problems is what to do with all its people. Another is how to grow enough food to feed so large a population.

There is another interesting feature of Japan's geography. Between Honshu, Shikoku and Kyushu is a part of the sea which is almost landlocked. This means that this part of the sea is almost surrounded by land, which is why it is called the Inland Sea. The eastern entrance to the Inland Sea is at a place called the Straits of Shimonoseki. It is so narrow that it has been possible to build a railway tunnel under the water at this point.

Now let's look at the map once again to find out something

14

about Japan's neighbours. To the west, on the mainland of Asia, lie Korea and a part of the U.S.S.R. known as Siberia. China lies to the south-west and only about 800 kilometres (500 miles) away. A long chain of small islands extends south from Japan, all the way to Taiwan (Formosa) which is about 2,000 kilometres (1,300 miles) away. These islands are known as the Ryukyu Islands, and the biggest and best-known of them is called Okinawa. It was on Okinawa that one of the Second World War's fiercest battles was fought between Japanese and American soldiers. It was returned to Japan in May 1972.

There are many fine modern cities in Japan. This is part of Tokyo

There are more islands to the north of Japan. The largest is Sakhalin. Most of the other northern islands belong to the Kurile group. It is just a short distance from the northern tip of Hokkaido to the nearest Russian-held territory—Sakhalin.

Finally, across the Pacific Ocean to the east, is the United States. We do not think of Japan as a close neighbour to America. The Pacific is a broad and often stormy ocean. But actually Tokyo is only nine hours away from the American west coast if you travel by jet.

We can understand how completely Japan was defeated during the Second World War when we learn that many of the nearby places we have mentioned belonged to Japan. Japan controlled Korea, Okinawa and all the Ryukyu Islands, even the big and very rich island of Formosa (now Taiwan). At one time during the war, Japanese soldiers attacked and occupied some of the Aleutian Islands which are a part of Alaska.

All of these possessions were lost when Japan was defeated. Several million Japanese who had lived in Korea and Formosa, and also in parts of China occupied by Japanese soldiers, had to go back home. This made the Japanese islands more crowded than ever.

Besides overcrowding, the Japanese have other troubles. We have mentioned earthquakes. In addition, violent storms called typhoons often hit Japan. These storms begin in the middle of the Pacific Ocean. Then they move north-west.

The typhoon season is from late summer to late autumn, and these storms often hit the Japanese islands with terrible winds

Part of the coast line of the Inland Sea

and rain. Huge waves wash into the little fishing villages along the coast. We know that rivers in mountainous country are short and swift. Such rivers become quickly flooded. Sometimes whole villages are swept away.

In the western world typhoons, like hurricanes, used to be given girls' names, each in sequence beginning with a letter of the alphabet. The first typhoon of the season might be called Alice, the next Betty, and so on. Today typhoons are given numbers instead, or place names.

A very bad typhoon—Kanogawa typhoon—struck the island of Honshu (at a place named Kanogawa) in 1958 and caused the death of nearly one thousand people.

Now we know something about Japan's geography and climate. The land area is small, and the population is large. There are mountains everywhere, and there are many volcanoes, some of which are still active. Because of the steep mountains, it is difficult for Japan to grow enough food. Because the islands are so crowded, the Japanese must be good businessmen. A modern people who lack arable land must rely on industry in order to prosper. So the Japanese have built many factories in order to make things for themselves and for sale to other countries.

Unloading the catch

The mountains of Japan cause other problems. It is expensive to build roads in mountainous country. And small islands with many mountains can have only short and swift rivers. These rivers are not deep enough for ships to use.

As we might suppose from the fact that all Japanese live quite close to the sea, fishing is an important industry. We shall learn that fish and other products of the sea are very important to the Japanese.

Japan's geography, which causes millions of people to be crowded into a small area, has had much to do with its history. Mostly because they lived on islands, the Japanese were shut off from the rest of Asia for many centuries. However, in modern times, the Japanese have waged four wars against their neighbours in order to try to get more living space and more economic prosperity for her people.

Cities which were rapidly rebuilt after the end of the Second World War have today grown to many times their pre-war size. Huge modern factories, manned by computers and robots, are commonplace. The railways run efficiently to provide rapid communication, and a countrywide network of roads has been established and is continually being improved.

Japan plays a full part in the modern world.

The First Japanese

We know that the Japanese, like the Chinese and Koreans, belong to a race of people we call Oriental. Often we use the word *yellow* to describe them and other Mongolian peoples as compared to the white, red, brown or black races.

Some of the early inhabitants of Japan were not, in fact, Orientals. They were called the Ainu. They came to Japan, many centuries ago, probably from Siberia. They nay have belonged to the Caucasian branch of the human family. The Ainu spread through the eastern part of Japan. Today there are only about 15,000 Ainu and they all live on Hokkaido Island. Our picture shows two Ainu girls. On another page you can see a picture of two Ainu men.

Ainu children of Northern Japan

Just as the Indians in North America were pushed westward by the pioneer settlers, the Ainu were slowly pushed north by other peoples who came to the Japanese islands. These new arrivals came from the south and west. Most of them were Orientals and they were quite different from the Ainu in appearance and customs.

Some of these Oriental people came from Central Asia, through Korea or China. Others came from the Philippines. Some of these settlers belonged to the Malay division of the human family, and came from as far away as the Malay Peninsula and the islands of Indonesia. Of course, this happened thousands of years ago.

These people came by boat and were probably hunters and fishermen. It is thought that they first settled on Kyushu Island. As the years passed, they spread slowly northward to Shikoku,

Honshu and, finally, away up to the northern island of Hokkaido.

At first the arrivals from the south and west settled along the coasts. As they increased in numbers, they moved into the mountains. Many became farmers. In time, even in Hokkaido these people whom we call the Japanese outnumbered the Ainu.

Most of the people of Japan are therefore Oriental, but with a mixture of Malay and, possibly, Polynesian blood too. They came to Japan from distant places. Probably some of Japan's early settlers came from as far away as New Guinea, the island to the north of Australia.

The Japanese developed their own language and customs.

**Two Ainu
from
Hokkaido**

For a long time they had little contact with their Chinese and Korean neighbours on the mainland of Asia. They became as different from Chinese and Koreans as people in North America are different from the Spanish-speaking peoples of South America.

The Japanese arrived on their islands several thousands of years ago. They were not then a great seafaring people, nor were they traders. They had no written language for a long time.

We might say that the Japanese were more backward than either the Chinese or Koreans. The earliest written record in Japanese goes back to A.D. 712, or nearly 1,300 years ago. But Chinese history goes back many centuries earlier.

According to the early records, the Sun Goddess sent her grandson to earth to become Japan's first ruler. This was supposed to have occurred in the year 660 B.C. This first ruler's name was Jimmu Tenno. All of Japan's Emperors are supposed to be direct descendants of Jimmu Tenno. The present Emperor is the 124th descendant.

The story about the Sun Goddess explains several things. The flag of Japan is a red ball on a white ground, and this represents the sun. The Japanese name for their country is *Ni-hon* which loosely means "Land of the Rising Sun". This word, said quickly, becomes *Nippon,* often used as a name for the country. Sometimes we speak of the Japanese as the Nipponese.

Korean and Chinese Influences

Hundreds of years before the time of Christ, China was a great and powerful nation. The Emperors of China ruled much of eastern Asia, and Chinese traders sailed far and wide in their junks. The Chinese had a written language. They had a religion called Buddhism, which had come to China from India. Chinese ideas, religion and art had spread to other parts of Asia including Korea.

Now let's look at the map of Japan again. We can see that Korea and Japan are separated by a narrow part of the sea called the Korean Straits. About the year A.D. 57, it is said, Japanese envoys, or representatives, crossed these straits and visited the court of the Korean King.

The Koreans had already received many ideas from China.

A powerful kingdom called the Silla had been established in the south-eastern part of the Korean peninsula. By the year A.D. 668 the Silla Kings controlled all of Korea. We can understand that Korea was a powerful nation when we know that in 613 the Koreans had fought and won a great war with China.

The Koreans had built many beautiful temples, monasteries and pagodas, and the Silla capital at Kyungju was a great centre of culture and learning. The first Japanese official envoy is thought to have visited Korea and China in A.D. 57. During the centuries which followed, Chinese as well as Korean civilization continued to be introduced into Japan. One of the most remarkable results of these contacts with Korea was perhaps

A seventeenth-century castle

The Japanese are fine craftsmen. This wood carving is in a shrine at Nikko

the big *Kofun*, or burial mound in memory of the Emperor Nintoku. This huge Kofun, which is as large as a park, is said to be the world's largest burial mound.

Historical records say that in these ancient times, Chinese

The Kinkaku-Ji temple in Kyoto

and Korean scholars wrote many books on Japan. Buddhism is also believed to have been introduced into Japan from Korea. We can think of Korea, therefore, as a bridge across which new ideas and a new religion came to Japan.

One of the most important things received from China was a form of picture writing. The Japanese still use these characters today; but, as we shall learn later, there are two other ways in which Japanese people write.

27

Two Great Cities

You may think that the Emperor Nintoku, who was honoured by having one of the world's largest tombs, and his successor the Emperor Ojin must always have been strong rulers. At first, in fact, the emperor was merely the chief of one of the "clans" who were fighting for power. Gradually, one of these clans, the Yamato, became all-powerful. It was the members of the Yamato family, ancestors of the present Japanese Imperial Family, who established Japan's first permanent capital.

This capital was first located at Nara and named Heijokyo. Nara, as it is now called, is one of the most beautiful cities in Japan. If you want to see Japanese temples, Nara is the best place to visit. There are hundreds of temples and pagodas there,

The shogun's castle, Tokyo, later the Imperial Palace

all surrounded by green hills. There is also a park in Nara where small deer roam and feed on the grass.

Buddhism, which flourished in the Nara period, encouraged the fine arts. The nine thousand art treasures in the Shosoin

Imperial Repository (which stands in the grounds of the Todaiji Temple) are the most representative of this period. They include costumes, accessories, weapons, musical instruments and furniture, all associated with the Emperor Shomu who founded the temple.

Politics in Nara were much disturbed by the growth of Buddhist influence. In 794 the Emperor moved the capital to the north in order to break the court's association with strong Buddhist sects. This new capital was called Heiankyo, "City of Peace". The present city of Kyoto has developed from it.

The life of the Imperial Court in Heiankyo was peaceful and colourful. The court ladies glided through the palace corridors dressed in twelve-fold silk garments.

The nobles enjoyed dancing, reciting poetry and writing; they wrote remarkably fine poetry and novels in both the Chinese and Japanese languages. The men preferred to write in Chinese; so the masterpieces of Japanese literature were mostly written by women. The most famous writer of this period was Lady Murasaki, a court lady who wrote a novel of great length. This describes the life of a Prince named Genji, and tells us much of the ideas and way of life of that time.

The Daibutsu or Buddha of Kamakura, erected in A.D. 1252

The Samurai and Kamikaze

While court nobles in Kyoto indulged in poetry, writing and the fine arts, life in the countryside became more difficult. The poverty of the peasants and the activities of a number of robber bands disturbed the landowners' peace. Some feudal lords began to maintain private armies and their soldiers became known as *Samurai*.

After a long period of unrest and many battles, a ruler named Yoritomo emerged. With the title of Shogun, he ruled from

A Japanese boy studying Buddhism at an early age

Kamakura, which is now famous for the Daibutsu, a large image of Buddha cast in bronze.

Meanwhile, relations between Japan and China, which had remained peaceful, suddenly changed. In 1274, over nine hundred ships, carrying a Mongol army supported by Korean troops, sailed for Japan. Some were sunk by storms but the Japanese were caught unawares by the sudden attack and by the new weapons of the Mongols, although they finally managed to drive them back.

The Mongols reappeared in 1281. But, one night, a great typhoon (which the Japanese called *Kamikaze* or "God-sent Wind") caught the Mongol ships and most of them were sunk or wrecked.

After the fall of the Kamakura government there was chaos, and civil wars followed. Finally, a strong man named Hideyoshi unified the country. He was the son of a humble peasant. Since his face resembled that of a monkey, many people called him "General Monkey". Hideyoshi, although a great general, was not a clever negotiator. The Ming rulers of China refused his request for official trade between the two countries. He also failed to achieve his ambition to conquer China with the aid of Korea. Following his death, the lords *(Daimyo)* of the eastern provinces defeated his successor who was supported by the lords of the western provinces. Then Tokugawa Ieyasu became Shogun. His family ruled Japan from 1600 to the middle of the nineteenth century.

In spite of the wars and general confusion, several cultural developments emerged at this time. They included the beginnings of *Kabuki* drama, and the Tea Ceremony. Drinking tea became a ceremony; both the guest and the host had to observe rules. Before drinking you had to eat a piece of cake and some sweetmeats; and at the end of the ceremony you had to turn your tea-cup upside down and look at it. This ceremony still survives today.

The famous city of Nikko is a memorial to the Shoguns of this period. Some of the most colourful temples and shrines in Japan are located here.

Opening Closed Doors

In the sixteenth century Portugal sent her ships and traders to many foreign shores. They traded with Korea and also established (in 1542) a trading-post at Macao on the coast of southern China. For a time Portuguese from Macao were allowed to trade with Japan. And in 1543, three Portuguese visited Japan. In 1549, Francisco Xavier (a Spanish Jesuit missionary later known as St. Francis Xavier) arrived in Japan to try to convert the Japanese to Christianity.

Other European traders were interested in Japan. A Dutch merchant ship, the *Liefde*, visited the country in 1600, and Ieyasu later employed the captain and the English pilot, William Adams, as advisers on matters of trade.

At first, Christianity was tolerated and soon many people were converted in southern Japan. Trade with European countries grew and the Tokugawa government issued passports to foreign merchants.

But later the Tokugawa Shoguns became suspicious and fearful of Christianity. They discouraged foreign traders because of their possible use as a means to colonise Japan. Ieyasu expelled all Europeans from Japan. By the 1620s he had also closed all ports, except Hirado and Nagasaki, to foreign ships. Then the Tokugawa family were informed by foreign merchants that Spanish and Portuguese missionaries had been secretly entering Japan. In 1622, a large number of these missionaries and their Japanese converts were killed.

This policy of closing Japan's doors to foreigners continued for more than two hundred years. It was not until 1853 that the doors were suddenly opened again. In that year, an American sailed into Japanese waters with four warships. He was Commodore Matthew Perry. His ships visited the tiny port of Shimoda on the Izu peninsula, south-west of Tokyo. The Japanese were frightened when they saw the huge American warships. They called them "black ships" because they had steam engines and thick black smoke came out of their funnels.

Tokyo as it looked in 1890

A view of modern Tokyo, a city filled with factories

The arrival of these "black ships" changed the history of Japan. There were many young *Samurai* who realised that Japan could no longer shut herself off from the world or from new ideas. The Tokugawa government soon fell, and a new group seized power and established the Emperor Meiji.

These new leaders appreciated the technological advances made by Western nations. They were also aware of the fate of Japan's neighbours, especially China, in the middle of the nineteenth century.

The new government started modernization plans with the slogan "Enrich the Nation and Strengthen the Army". The *Samurai* and feudal lords gave up their inherited power. A national army (modelled on that of Germany) and a navy (modelled on the British Navy) were formed. The country was

37

divided into prefectures, which were like separate states; and, in 1868, the capital was moved from Kyoto to Tokyo.

The Emperor accepted a Constitution providing for a House of Representatives and a House of Peers; this legislative body was to be called the Diet. There was also a Cabinet, headed by a Prime Minister. However, the ordinary people still played very little part in the government of the country. A government elected by a narrow section of the population (and, above all, the Cabinet) had, in the name of the Emperor, virtually complete power over the lives of the Japanese people.

In 1872, the first Japanese railway (connecting Tokyo with the port of Yokohama) was built. Other railways soon followed. Japanese ships began to sail far and wide and large factories were built in many Japanese cities.

The Emperor Meiji was a strong ruler but his successor, the Emperor Taisho (who reigned from 1912 to 1925) was little more than a figurehead. Things became even worse in the reign of the next young emperor when the government was gradually taken over by military leaders who were determined to dominate Asia. In 1932, the Japanese army occupied Manchuria, setting up a puppet state which was named Manchukuo. In 1937, they attempted an invasion of northern China.

In 1939, the Second World War began. Japan's generals and admirals thought that if they joined in this war between the great nations of Europe they might get a chance to strike in other parts of Asia. And so, in 1941, Japan attacked the United States.

After the Second World War Japan began a period of reconstruction. This view of Tokyo shows how the modernization has continued since then

War and Reconstruction

On December 7th, 1941, Japanese planes bombed Pearl Harbour in the Hawaiian Islands, destroying a large part of the American Pacific Fleet. And within a few months the Japanese had occupied most of the islands of the Central and South Pacific.

But the military leaders of Japan made a mistake: they did not understand the great industrial might of America. They told their own people that Japan was protected by the Emperor and could not be conquered.

Slowly, American forces moved closer to Japan, retaking island after island. Meanwhile, Western scientists were developing a new and terrible weapon—an atomic bomb. This new weapon was successfully tested and ready for use in the summer of 1945.

On the morning of August 6th, 1945, a single American B-29 plane flew high over Hiroshima. The atomic bomb was dropped. On August 9th the city of Nagasaki was hit by a second bomb.

On September 2nd, 1945, the American battleship *Missouri* sailed into Tokyo Bay, and General Douglas MacArthur,

This is what the atomic bomb which was dropped on Hiroshima looked like from the air

representing the United States of America and the Allies, accepted the complete surrender of Japan.

Japan was immediately occupied by Allied soldiers, for the most part Americans. A military government was established. The American occupation lasted for six years. During this time, the Japanese way of life was turned upside-down. Schools were reorganized and textbooks were rewritten. A new Constitution was drawn up, giving new powers to the Japanese people. Political parties were organized and elections were held in which everyone, including women, could vote.

At the same time, the Japanese were rebuilding their bombed and burnt cities, their factories and railways, which had been mostly destroyed. In 1951, a peace treaty was signed. It was an unusual treaty because, by that time, most of the bitterness of the war had been forgotten.

It is virtually impossible today to find any reminder of wartime damage in Japan, except in Hiroshima where one of the few buildings left standing after the atomic explosion has been retained to draw attention to the horrors of modern warfare.

We have learned of Japan's past, let us now see how the Japanese live today in cities and in the country, what crops they grow, what food they eat, and how the children go to school.

If You Were a Japanese Boy or Girl . . .

I took my two sons and one daughter to Japan. They were surprised by many things. We slept on the floor and in houses which had only paper sliding doors between rooms. We had fish, either raw or cooked, at almost every meal. We ate with chopsticks, as do most of the people in the Orient. We did not ride in, or even see, a rickshaw, or as it is sometimes called, *jin-rickshaw*, although this man-pulled carriage was invented in Japan. Nowadays a Japanese boy or girl who saw a rickshaw in Tokyo would be as surprised as any boy or girl of the Western world. Rickshaws are still used in many other countries; but in Japan people travel in buses, taxis, trains and planes; there are also thousands of motorcycles, and plenty of bicycles.

Japanese railways are among the best in the world. It is un-

A typical Japanese family at home—western style!

usual for a Japanese train to be even a few minutes late. Big buses go to every corner of the country.

In other words, Japan is a very modern country. Yet there are different and interesting ways of living and doing things in Japan.

Japanese houses are different from any others in Asia. The Japanese sleep on the floor as do Koreans. But Koreans have heated floors, called *ondals*. Japanese floors are covered with heavy rush mats, called *tatami*.

At one time, there was very little furniture in most Japanese homes. The family sat on the floor and ate at a low table. Heavy quilts were kept in large cupboards with sliding doors. At night-time, they were taken out and spread on the floor for the family to sleep on or use as covers. In those days, many houses were heated only with charcoal—which was burned in a large pot called a *hibachi*.

Today, however, the typical Japanese home is well-heated (often by gas) and is usually fully furnished in western style.

My children often forgot one thing that is very important. You must take your shoes off before going into a Japanese home or hotel. Shoes would scuff and soil the tatami. So, if you were a Japanese boy or girl, you'd take off your shoes at the front door and put on slippers. The hallways are made of wood, and it is all right to walk on these if you are wearing slippers. Then, when you get to the tatami rooms, off go the slippers.

It is so necessary to take off your shoes, and it must be done so many times each day, that many Japanese carry shoehorns with them. Often Japanese businessmen have shoehorns stuck in their breast pockets, just as we sometimes carry pencils or pens. For the same reason, many do not wear shoes. Instead they wear a kind of slippers called *geta* which may be removed quickly.

Japanese houses are attractive. There is sometimes a little nook in the living-room called a *tokonoma*, where there will always be some flowers, beautifully arranged. And, even though it may be very small, there is nearly always a little garden.

Japanese and Chinese who have lived in the West sometimes

say jokingly that a man would be in heaven if he lived in a Western-style house, had a Chinese cook and a Japanese wife. The Western house with central heating and many conveniences; Chinese food, which is so good; and a Japanese wife, who lives to serve her husband—these would make a perfect combination!

This brings us to the food you would eat if you were a Japanese boy or girl. The average Japanese family today eats a mixture of foods of Japanese, Chinese and western origin. Japanese food is not considered by most other nations to be as good as Chinese food, or even as good as Korean food. Like their Chinese and Korean neighbours, the Japanese eat rice. It is their most important food. They used to have rice for breakfast, rice for lunch, rice for dinner. But today many Japanese also vary their diet with bread and pasta.

The next most important part of the diet is fish. The Japanese eat fish cooked, fish that has been dried and salted—and fish raw! The raw fish is eaten in slices *(sashimi)* which are sometimes dipped in a mixture of soy sauce and grated horseradish. Japanese food includes many other products of the sea—as well as seaweed. This is dried and served in little waferlike squares, or prepared in a number of other ways.

Pickles form the third important part of a traditional Japanese meal. There are different kinds of pickles. One of the most popular is called *taku-an*, and is made from turnips.

Along with rice, fish, seaweed and other products of the sea, there is nearly always one soup with each meal. Often the soup is made from bean curd and fish. Sometimes it may be made

Modern Japanese houses

with strips of pork, or perhaps a fishhead. And always there is tea. Tea is the national drink of Japan.

There are several Japanese dishes that foreigners enjoy. *Sukiyaki* is the best known, and there are sukiyaki restaurants in some big American cities. This dish is made from strips of beef, several different vegetables, bean curd and noodles, all cooked at the table in a sauce made from soy beans and sugar.

Another famous Japanese dish is *tempura,* made from fish, shrimps and vegetables which are put in thick batter and fried in deep fat. There are hundreds of tempura places in Tokyo and other big Japanese cities. The food is cooked behind a counter, right in front of the customer. Bean-curd soup and rice are added to make a filling meal.

In cities, another popular restaurant dish is *yakitori* which is really barbecued chicken. The chicken is cut into small pieces, put on a spit and roasted with wonderful sauce.

Japanese food is always nice to look at. In other words, it is attractively prepared, served in different-shaped dishes. Sometimes it seems that the cook spends more time trying to make the meal beautiful than making it tasty. But this is a part of the Japanese love of beauty. It is expressed in many ways, even in the preparing and serving of meals.

There is a saying about Oriental people that tells us something about the Japanese. It says: "The Japanese wash their bodies, while the Koreans wash their clothes." The Japanese probably take more baths than any other people in the world. And a Japanese bath is so hot that foreigners often get burned stepping into a Japanese bath tub.

A meal being served in a traditional Japanese house. (Note the chopsticks)

In traditional Japanese homes the bath is made of wood, and a boiler heats the water for it. But in Japan you do not actually bathe in this kind of bath. That would be very impolite! First, you soap yourself; then the soap is washed off, outside the bath; only then do you get into the bath—to soak.

We have already read that there are many hot springs in Japan. There are about 700 villages and cities that have natural hot springs. The water is piped straight into homes and inns. Japanese love to go to a hot-springs inn for a weekend or holiday. Many rooms in hot-springs inns have big private hot baths. And each inn has a large community bath where from a dozen to one hundred people can soak at one time.

A more western-style home—even here the family are eating with chopsticks

A Japanese lady and little girl in traditional kimono and "obi", or sash, worshipping at a shrine. A Seven-Five-Three Festival scene

Notice the picture of the Japanese lady. She is dressed in the kimono and *obi* which were once worn by all Japanese women. Men also wore a loose-fitting kimono. The old manner of dress is quite different from either Chinese or Korean and is very beautiful. However, most Japanese now wear Western-style dress except for festivals and special ceremonies.

Young Japanese have copied many Western ways. The girls

Japanese children
in festive and
traditional clothes

and young women wear dresses and high heels. They love to dance and to hear jazz music.

Of course in the country and in small towns one still sees many Japanese dressed as in olden days. But the ways are changing, although in recent years there has been a revival in the fashion for kimonos to wear at weddings, funerals, and other ceremonial occasions.

Going to School

Japan is one of the most literate countries in the world. This means that almost every Japanese can read. Having a good education is important in Japan, and almost all boys and girls go to school.

For a while after the end of the Second World War (1939–45), all boys and girls wore school uniforms. This was considered democratic because poor children and rich children all dressed

Schoolchildren in western clothes. Traditional Japanese clothes are usually worn on special occasions

alike. However, wearing of uniforms now depends on the school. In many schools uniforms are worn. The girls have blouses and skirts, and the boys wear black uniforms and caps. There are also many school children, especially in the country, who do not wear uniforms.

Japanese children study much the same subjects as you do in school. Until 1945, they had to learn much about serving the Emperor and following a warlike code of behaviour called

Uniformed Japanese schoolboys enjoy a festival day

Bushido. A good student had to be able to recite the names of every one of Japan's 124 Emperors! Now all this has changed. But Japanese boys and girls must still learn to write Japanese in *three different ways.* This is just as if we had three different alphabets and had to learn to write with each one!

Remember that the Japanese learned the Chinese way of writing centuries ago when Chinese and Korean scholars came to Japan. Chinese is a kind of picture writing. There are thousands of different characters, each with a different meaning. In order to read a newspaper, one must learn nearly 2,000 characters. If you were to visit Tokyo, you'd notice that most of the signs along the streets are in Chinese characters. But often there are other marks in addition to the Chinese characters. These are in other forms of writing called Hiragana and Katakana.

The Japanese had no system of writing before A.D. 400, when Chinese characters were first used. Then Katakana was invented in about A.D. 800, and is now used to write the names of foreign places and people. Hiragana was invented about a hundred years later. In modern Japanese language reform sponsored by the government, Katakana and Hiragana are used in conjunction with about 1,850 Chinese characters. Imagine having to learn to read three different writings at the same time! No wonder Japanese school children are industrious.

In Japan, reading begins on the right, and goes from top to bottom. This being so, the front cover of a Japanese book would be the back cover of a book printed in English. Nowadays, however, some books have the words arranged in Western style, from left to right.

When Japanese children first go to school they learn Katakana. This is a *phonetic* (or "sound") alphabet of 47 different letters or signs. Each sign means a sound. By putting the signs together, it is possible to write a word. This phonetic alphabet is studied first because it is not hard to learn.

It is after Japanese children have learned to write phonetically that they must begin to study Kanji, or Chinese characters. This is much more difficult. As we have mentioned, this means knowing about 2,000 characters. And a real scholar needs to learn many more characters. Knowing how to read and write characters is hard work!

The Koreans have the same system of writing. They also have their own simple alphabet called Hangul but they too use Chinese characters. Most Korean newspapers and books are printed in mixed script with Hangul and Chinese mixed up on the same page or in the same sentence. Japanese newspapers, books and street signs are also often written in mixed script.

After learning Katakana and beginning to learn Chinese characters, Japanese children also learn Hiragana. This, as we have said, is another phonetic alphabet. Then, of course, they must learn to put together the different ways of writing in mixed script!

Our picture shows some Japanese writing. In the top two lines most of the words are in Chinese. But there are four peculiar-looking squiggles around which I have drawn circles.

海上飛行中緊急事故の
場合に於ける心得

海上不時着の時の心得

航海なさる場合に救命具の事に就いてよく慣らされると同じに航空機に乗られた場合も万一に備へて避難又は機を放棄す時の處置を知つて置く事は賢明な事と存じます。この説明書

These are in Hiragana. You can see that the phonetic script is quite different from the Chinese characters. The characters are printed with many strokes that are generally straight. Hiragana is printed with simpler, flowing strokes.

Look at the other lines. Can you separate the Chinese characters from the Hiragana? When they are handwritten it is not so easy to see which is which, unless you know them!

Even though Chinese characters are used by the Japanese, the spoken language is entirely different from Chinese. However, there are quite a few words that come from China. These are called Chinese derivative words. There are also many words that come from English.

When Japan suddenly decided to become a modern nation

A Japanese calligraphy
teacher showing a girl
how to write

of factories, railways and cars, new words were needed. Instead
of finding Japanese words to express new ideas, the Japanese
often took English words and used them. More English words
were added during the years when there were thousands of
American soldiers occupying Japan.

Most Japanese words end in a vowel or the letter "N". When
they took English words in their vocabulary, the Japanese
generally added the letter "U" or "O" to the word. A bed is
called "bedo". To back, as in reversing a car, is "backu". There
is no "L" sound in Japanese, and English words with "L" were
changed to have a rolled "R" sound. Baseball, a game the
Japanese love, is called "Basu-boru". There are hundreds of
English words used in everyday Japanese.

As with so many other things, we can see how the Japanese
have borrowed from other nations, copied, and added to make
something just right for them. They took China's written language but invented simpler alphabets needed to express all
sounds and ideas. They added some Chinese words to Japanese,

and later added English words for new ideas and new things.

All educated Japanese speak the same language, called the Tokyo dialect. But there are many differences in spoken Japanese. The Japanese spoken in southern Kyushu is so different from that spoken in northern Honshu that people cannot understand each other. When with their families, or if visiting their home town, Japanese will speak their local dialects. But business, government and education are conducted in the Tokyo dialect that all Japanese can speak.

Perhaps we can understand another reason why Japan has become a great modern nation before China. The Chinese have an even greater number of dialects, but successive Chinese governments have always had a difficult time getting all Chinese to learn and speak one national language. There are still many Chinese who cannot speak Mandarin, which is the name of China's national language. The disciplined Japanese, used to following orders, learned to speak one dialect when told to do so, more particularly because Tokyo was the centre for business and government.

We will find that this is one great difference between the Japanese and other peoples in Asia. The idea of complete loyalty, of obeying authority, even of giving one's life without question—this way of thinking has made the Japanese a disciplined people. Whether told to learn one national dialect or to die for the Emperor, they have obeyed.

Respect for authority also shows itself in the way people talk. Many centuries ago, the Japanese began to use the word "honourable" when addressing their parents or grandparents.

This way of speaking has been used for so long that the Japanese do not even realize what they are saying. This helps us understand another national trait, especially about Japanese children at home and in school. The Japanese are among the most *formal* people in the world. There is a *right* way to do everything in Japan, from addressing one's neighbour to serving dinner.

When Japanese people meet in the street there is a great deal of bowing. Everyone bows to everyone, and it seems that each person is trying to bow a little lower than the others, or trying to bow more often. Sometimes the bowing goes on, up and down, for five minutes.

But as with so many other things, this outward politeness is also changing. Among young Japanese, there is much less of the formality that has long been a part of Japanese life. Japanese young people are becoming more and more like young people in Western countries.

Japanese children are still taught to love their country but in a different way from in the past. It is no longer necessary to know the names of all 124 Emperors or to believe that the Emperor is divine. But Japanese children know a great deal about their country. Each autumn, during October, Japanese schools close for a day—or several days. Then the whole school goes on field trips. Travelling by bus or train, the children visit Japan's historic spots, the national parks, the famous mountains.

During October it is difficult to get a room in a Japanese inn

Schoolchildren in a primary school playground

because so many boys and girls are out seeing their country. Those who cannot go on long trips visit all the important places in their home cities.

Fish made from dyed cotton cloth flying over a farmer's house on Boys' Day

Games, Festivals and Religion

Japan is a land of many festivals. There are beautiful festivals in connection with religious or important past events. We'll read about these, but first let's learn about some special children's games and festivals.

One of our pictures shows some big cotton fish flying in the breeze. In another picture three little girls, all dressed in an old Japanese style, are having tea in front of a big collection of dolls.

First, let's look again at the picture of the fish. These are supposed to be carp, a special fish. Carp symbolize courage and endurance. Each year on the fifth day of the fifth month Boys' Day is celebrated. On that day you can look at many

60

A little girls' tea party, with dolls in the background

homes and tell how many boys there are in the family. Sometimes, one carp is flown for each boy. So there may be eight brothers living in the farmer's house below the fish in the picture. Often the fish for Boys' Day are flown for a couple of weeks before and after the actual day.

On Girls' Day, sets of dolls are brought out for display. The girls of the family dress up in their very best. They visit other little girls. Girls' Day is celebrated on March 3rd.

Japanese boys and girls have many games, some much like those we play. But the game which Japanese, young and old, love most is baseball! This is strange, isn't it? All over the world baseball is considered *the* American sport. Or perhaps we should call it the game of the Americas, because the people of Central and South America love the game too. As far as we know, there is only one other place besides Japan where baseball is played by so many people. That is in a part of Central Africa.

Baseball was introduced to a Japanese school in 1873 by two American teachers. The Japanese play the game according to exactly the same rules as are used in America. Professional teams use the same rules as the New York Yankees or the Milwaukee Braves. Yes, there are even professional teams in Japan. The Japanese have their own World Series. The players dress like American players, the umpires look just like American umpires. They shout "striku" and "boru" (for ball), and say "out" and "home run" (or a Japanese version of these terms).

Japanese baseball games are broadcast and televised. During

Japanese children celebrating on the first day of January by doing "New Year's writing"

World Series time, Japanese, rich and poor, try to find an excuse to get to the nearest TV set! That sounds like America, doesn't it? It is strange, isn't it, that America gave Japan one of its popular sports so many years ago.

Another unusual Japanese sport is called *sumo*. This is a kind of wrestling, but not at all like the matches we see on television. We think of the Japanese as small people, and they are generally smaller than Europeans. But Japanese wrestlers weigh as much as 130 kilogrammes (290 pounds). They must go through years of training—and eating. This sport is over 1,200 years old. Sumo wrestlers dress in a special manner, and wear their hair in a "topknot".

For the past three hundred years a Grand Champion Sumo wrestler, called a Yokozuna, has been crowned from time to time.

Each year there are big spring and summer sumo tournaments three of which are held in Tokyo. Season tickets may cost large sums of money.

On Shikoku Island, a special breed of sumo dog is raised. Called *tosa*, these dogs are very large, they are dressed like sumo wrestlers, and they really do wrestle.

Japanese children like pets. They love dogs, cats and goldfish. But they also enjoy some much smaller pets. Many crickets and fireflies are sold. There is a famous restaurant in Tokyo which

This is a sumo dog, or "tosa"

buys fireflies from all over Japan. Each evening from May 25th to June 25th fireflies are released in the restaurant garden and people enjoy watching the twinkling insects while they eat. This Tokyo restaurant buys one million fireflies each spring. Fireflies are also sold in pairs, in cages.

We should mention one other unusual pet, a bird that works for its living! Both in China and in Japan, fishermen train a bird called the cormorant to catch fish. Cormorants are long-necked water birds related to ducks and geese. The birds are on a leash. There is a ring round each bird's neck so that it cannot swallow the fish. The cormorants dive into the water from small boats, gobble up all the fish their big throats can hold, and then swim back to the boat. Today, this is mainly a tourist attraction but in the past it was a normal method of fishing.

There are many colourful festivals in Japan. Some are observed in connection with Buddhism and Shinto, the two ancient Japanese religions. Remember that before Japan was defeated, Japanese actually worshipped the Emperor as one of the most important Shinto gods. After the war, the Emperor told his people that he was not a god after all. He is still loved and respected. But Shinto is not the great religion it once was for most Japanese.

However, Japan's hundreds of Shinto shrines are still visited by thousands of Japanese. Many of the ancient Shinto religious festivals are still observed, perhaps as much for pleasure as for worship. Down through the centuries Buddhism and Shinto grew together and sometimes were mixed up. Often there are

A Japanese wedding ceremony

beautiful Shinto shrines and Buddhist temples next to each other.

We mentioned the Daibutsu, or Great Buddha of Kamakura, built in 1252, over two hundred years before Columbus discovered the New World. There are other important images of gods and goddesses, temples and shrines all over Japan.

Nara and Kyoto, both ancient capitals of Japan, are famous for their temples. Nikko, a small city in the mountains nearly 145 kilometres (ninety miles) north of Tokyo, is also a famous shrine city. These shrines were built by the Tokugawa rulers, and some of the famous shoguns are buried at Nikko.

There are many colourful festivals in connection with Japan's temples and shrines, or as a part of Japanese religion. Let's mention just a few of these.

A traditional shrine in a woodland setting

One festival in which boys and girls take part is called the Seven-Five-Three Festival. Traditionally, girls who become three years old and seven years old and boys who become three or five are dressed up in their very best on November 15th. Then their parents take them to the nearest Shinto shrine to pray to all the many Shinto gods. Nowadays, however, some people take their children (either boys or girls) at any age.

The picture shows Japanese girls celebrating a different sort of festival. They are carrying a portable shrine called an *omikoshi*. Perhaps you can see that this festival is more for fun than anything else. The girls seem to be having a good time!

Girls carrying an "omikoshi" in one of Japan's many festivals

Each year on July 7th there is a Star Festival. People write poems to the stars. These are written on strips of coloured paper and fastened to bamboo poles. Streets are decorated with banners, lanterns and bunting. In August there is another important festival called the Feast of the Lanterns. This honours the dead.

In some cities there are special festivals, like the Gion Festival which takes place each summer in Kyoto. Certain temples and shrines have special days. On October 17th and May 17th there is a great festival and procession to the Toshogu Shrine in Nikko. Unfortunately we do not have space to write about all of Japan's many festivals.

We have learned that some of these are especially for children. And children have fun during all the festivals. Temples, shrines and even whole cities are gaily decorated. There seems to be some kind of special observance somewhere in Japan on almost every day of the year.

As we have said, the number of people who are true believers in Buddhism or Shinto is not as great as it once was. Among old people there are still many who visit the shrines to worship.

Christmas is widely celebrated by the Japanese. The shops in the cities have Christmas trees and decorations. Many people exchange gifts. This is not because there are a great many Christians. Only about one per cent of the people are Christians, but this small number includes many important people. Remember that there have been Christians in Japan for nearly

Schoolchildren choosing goldfish to buy

400 years. Remember too that the Japanese are imitators and easily absorb outside ideas.

Life in the Country

Tokyo is now one of the world's largest metropolitan areas, with a population of nearly twelve million. There are many other large cities. Osaka, which is also on Honshu, is Japan's second city with over three million people. Nagoya is the third city with a two million population. Other important cities are the ports of Yokohama, Kobe and Nagasaki.

But Japan is also a land of small villages and farms. Both fishing and farming are important. We might have guessed this when we learned that the Japanese eat a great deal of fish and rice. Rice is perhaps the most important crop. It is grown in terraced fields which must be irrigated. This means that the fields which are known as paddy-fields must have a constant supply of water.

The Japanese grow all the rice they need. Because so much of Japan is almost straight-up-and-down mountains this is a difficult problem. Japanese farmers are very clever at making terraces on steep slopes; but there are many mountains so steep that farming is impossible.

Rice is the most important food crop. This is a paddy field

There are other important crops, including many varieties of vegetables. Remember that the Japanese like pickled vegetables, especially *taku-an* which is made from turnips. We have also learned that the Japanese like to drink tea. Japanese farmers grow a great deal of tea, which comes from small bushes. Most of Japan's tea is what we call green tea. Among other Japanese crops are fruits, including apples, pears, peaches, plums, loquats, persimmons and strawberries. In southern Japan, citrus fruits such as oranges and tangerines are grown.

In addition, there are battery chickens, Scandinavian-type pig farms and cattle-raising in Hokkaido, as well as on the lower slopes of volcanic mountains and on river banks in the other islands.

The American Occupation changed the life of Japan's farmers. Until Japan was defeated, most farmers did not own their own land. They were tenant farmers. This means that they rented the land from landowners. Often the yearly rent was so high it was not possible to have much left over to provide for one's family.

During the Occupation, there was a land reform programme. All the tenant farmers who wished to do so could buy land from their landlords. Payment could be made over a long period of years. Thousands of farmers did buy land and became their own landlords.

The farmers of Japan have prospered. There is always need for more food. Many Japanese farmers have been able to buy tractors and other modern farm equipment. Their wives have refrigerators and washing machines. Just as Japan's business-men were quick to learn new ways after Commodore Perry opened Japan's doors, so the farmers have learned to farm with modern methods. In this way, Japan's farmers are different from the farmers in other Asian countries. In China and South-east Asia, most farm work is still done by hand. But in Japan there is more and more mechanical equipment. Instead of going to market in an ox-cart, a Japanese farmer is more likely to use a motorcycle or small truck.

In addition to rice, vegetables and tea, there are other crops. Some Japanese raise worms! But these worms are a very special variety. They spin beautiful threads of silk. The silkworm in-dustry is less important today than it used to be, because of the

Gathering the rice harvest

man-made fibres that can take the place of Japanese silk.

The Japanese began making silk in the year A.D. 794. The area around Kyoto is the centre of this industry. The silkworms are raised by Japanese families in the city and country. Factories in Kyoto make the raw silk into beautiful silk cloth. Japan produces more silk than any other country.

The Japanese are very good fishermen. We have mentioned the importance of fish in the Japanese diet. The Japanese also can fish and export it to other countries. In fishing, as in farming, we can see how the Japanese have raced ahead of their neighbours. Korean and Chinese fishermen still use many sailing boats called junks. But the Japanese have mechanized their fishing boats. In addition, they are very active fish farmers, breeding freshwater fish on a large scale.

The Japanese fish along their own coasts and in the Inland Sea. Deep-sea fishing vessels also sail far out into the Pacific and beyond, sometimes reaching waters far distant from their homes.

Twentieth-century Japan is a modern country. All the little fishing boats have motors

Cultured pearls,
a famous Japanese export

We have learned about one other product of the sea—the seaweed which is eaten by the Japanese. This is taken from the sea by divers. Another product that has become important also comes from the sea. Japanese cultured pearls are world-famous.

For centuries after pearls were first discovered, they were only found by chance. A pearl is produced sometimes when a bit of sand or tiny piece of coral gets inside the oyster. The pearl grows around this tiny particle. Divers went down into the sea, found oysters, and hoped there would be some with pearls inside.

In 1893, a famous Japanese named Kokichi Mikimoto developed a way to *make* pearls. He did this by *putting* something into the oyster. In other words, he did not wait for a pearl to begin forming naturally by chance. He took thousands of small oysters from the sea, and into each shell he put a grain of sand or some other tiny thing around which a pearl might form; then he put them back in the water to let pearls develop.

For many years other businessmen who sold pearls claimed that cultured pearls were not *real* pearls. But Mikimoto had experts come from other countries to study his methods and his "home-grown" pearl. The experts said that cultured pearls were not only real but just as beautiful as any other pearls.

The Mikimoto Pearl Farms are located on Ago Bay which is near the big city of Nagoya. There, and at other farms, oysters themselves are grown. Tiny edible oysters are "planted" in empty shells, and then put into the sea where they may be easily taken out again. Normally two or three years are required for an ordinary oyster to grow large enough to eat. But, by taking this short cut, the Japanese make their oysters ready to eat in less than a year.

Industry and Transportation

We have begun to understand some of Japan's problems. The islands of Japan are small in area but in population Japan is the seventh largest nation in the world. The mountainous islands cannot produce enough food for the population.

In order to keep strong and healthy, Japan must be a business nation. Since so much food must be bought from other countries, Japan must also make things that can be sold to other countries. Japanese leaders understood this when they decided to modernize

78

their country well over a hundred years ago. We have already learned how quickly railways, hydroelectric plants and factories were built.

Almost all Japanese factories were destroyed by bombing during the Second World War. But since that time these factories have been rebuilt. In addition many new industries have been started. Japan is again a great trading nation, selling its products to other countries throughout the world. Our pictures show some of the products of Japan's factories. Shipbuilding is very important. Japanese shipyards build freighters, ocean-going passenger liners and huge oil tankers. Japan has become the world's most important shipbuilding nation.

Japan builds its own railway locomotives and carriages. It produces and exports cars, trucks and motorcycles. In order to build such equipment, it is necessary to have steel. Japan's steel mills produce vast quantities of high-grade steel.

There are also some spinning mills in Japan. But the making of textiles is no longer one of Japan's important export industries.

In Japanese factories other whole new factories are built for sale to foreign countries. The Japanese make electrical equipment, including huge generators and turbines. A whole electric train has been made and exported to India. Japanese cameras, binoculars, microscopes, calculators, radios and televisions are sold all over the world. One company makes over 20,000 grand pianos for export each year.

From all this, we can understand that the Japanese are very

good businessmen. But they make many things besides heavy industrial products. Remember how Chinese and Korean artists came to teach the Japanese nearly 1,400 years ago. The Japanese learned then to become fine craftsmen. They learned to make earthenware and china. Now Japanese china is world-famous. There are several large factories in the city of Nagoya. Beautiful sets of crockery are made for export. For all these exports, the Japanese buy foodstuffs, as well as coal and iron ore—two things needed for the making of steel—from other countries.

The Japanese have been criticized because their factories only turn out copies of foreign goods. People say they can copy things made by other countries but cannot produce anything original. It has also been claimed that Japanese workmanship is not good. Perhaps in the past many Japanese goods were poorly made. But this is no longer true. Japanese businessmen have learned that they must make good products as well as products that can sell at a cheap price. So the quality of their exports has improved. In many fields, Japanese products have now surpassed those of other countries.

Japan must be an industrial and trading nation in order to remain strong. Because Japanese workmen are sometimes paid less than workers in Europe and America, it is often possible to sell Japanese goods at a cheaper price than those made in other countries.

Let's remember that at the end of the Second World War Japan was a ruined country. But in less than fifteen years the country had completely recovered from the war.

Japan is now the world's biggest shipbuilding nation

The Kurobe Dam, an example of Japanese engineering

An industrial nation must have a good transportation system. Japan has one of the best railway systems in the world. Most of the main lines are electrified. This means that there must be many power plants to produce the electricity needed, not only for the railways but for factories and cities as well. Japan's rivers, swiftly flowing through mountainous country, have been dammed in many places to produce hydroelectric, or water, power to meet some of these needs.

We have a saying about some railway lines: "You can set your watch by the trains." This is really true in Japan. The Japanese like to have everything exactly on time. If a train is supposed to leave at 11:03, it leaves at exactly 11:03. And Japanese trains are not only among the most punctual in the world; they are also very fast.

Building railways in Japan has been costly and difficult because of the mountains. There are hundreds of railway tunnels including one which goes under the Inland Sea to connect the Honshu and Kyushu islands. Even roads must often use tunnels to get through the mountains.

The Japanese are now trying to improve their road system. They have built some toll roads. (This means that people must pay to use the roads).

In spite of the improved road system, which includes high-speed motorways, Japanese cities have the same traffic problems as all other cities of the world. However, the buses are big and comfortable. And there are also thousands of taxicabs of many different sizes. In Japan, one pays for a taxi according to the size of the cab. A small taxi costs much less than a big one.

We might also expect that the Japanese, always quick to keep up with the world, would have excellent airlines. And they do. All the main cities of Japan are served by air. Japanese airliners fly throughout South-east Asia, as well as to Europe and the west coast of America. It is interesting that Japanese commercial planes now fly to many of the cities of Asia once occupied by the Japanese army.

But now the men who travel abroad are not soldiers but businessmen. There have been great changes in the relations between Japan and her neighbours. There is still some fear and distrust of the Japanese who tried to conquer all of Asia. But, for the most part, the other peoples of Asia feel that Japan has changed and that the Japanese will not make war on their neighbours again.

The Government of Modern Japan

Try and imagine any country suddenly changing its way of government. Instead of our present system, say we had a dictator with complete power. We would no longer elect our parliamentary representatives. Such a change is hard to imagine and would be very difficult to get used to. Yet a change just as great has taken place in Japan.

After surrender and during the American Occupation, Japan's government was completely changed. We have mentioned that

The Diet building in Tokyo, seat of Japan's government

the Emperor told his people that he was not really divine. The Emperor now has practically no power. Japan has become a constitutional monarchy very much like the United Kingdom.

There is still a Diet, as before. This is much the same as the British Houses of Parliament. The members of the Diet are elected by the people. There are political parties, just as in other democracies. The two largest parties are the Liberal-Democratic party and the Socialist party. There are several smaller parties including the Communist.

The Emperor appoints the Prime Minister who is the leader of the party which wins an election. In modern Japan, the Prime Minister has much more power than the Emperor. He in turn appoints the cabinet. The head of a department of government is called a Minister as in the British government.

There have been many other changes in Japan's government. Under the old system, the police were very powerful. Many Japanese were arrested without warrants, sometimes they were beaten, or imprisoned for years. There was no real freedom of speech, press or religion. Anyone who opposed the government might be arrested.

In modern Japan there is complete freedom of speech. Newspapers can, and very often do, criticize the government. And there is complete freedom of religion.

One aspect of
modern Japan
is its high
buildings and
crowded roads.
This is a typical
Tokyo scene

The constitution of Japan was rewritten during the American Occupation. The new constitution is much like the American Constitution. Yet it is unusual in one way. It states that Japan will never make war on any other nation. It even states that the Japanese government shall have no army, navy or air force, and that the right of the government to make war is not even recognized.

Japan is the only nation in the world to say that it will never make war again (although the country now has a Defence Force). That is certainly a change from the centuries during which Japanese followed *Bushido,* when it was honourable to be a warrior, to die for the Emperor.

This unusual section of Japan's new democratic constitution leads us to some of the problems faced by the people of Japan today.

Japan's Problems

Any small country with a large population has to face the basic problem of how to provide food and other necessities for its people. Japan, with about 112 million people, has always been conscious of overcrowding her islands and of the shortage of food and raw materials. Perhaps this is one reason why Japan went to war four times in fifty years. By controlling Korea, Formosa and much of China, Japan had a much larger area to rely on.

Although the mountainous islands of Japan make the cultivation of the land and the growing of food difficult, this is not now Japan's main problem. As we have read, Japan today is a

successful commercial and industrial power. To maintain this
commerce and industry (which, in turn, helps to provide the
food for her enormous population), Japan needs raw materials.
These she has to import, since the country is poor in natural
resources. Of course, buying raw materials for manufacture in

Soldiers of Japan's new army, called the Defence Force

Japan is just one link in the chain of Japan's relations with other countries in the world. Her trade with both Asian and Western countries involves the purchase of raw materials, the export of manufactured goods (the sale of which provides money for the purchase of yet more raw materials, as well as food) and also the purchase of essential goods for sale in Japan.

Japanese toys have long been famous in Europe and the western world. Now we can buy many other things from Japan which are sold in our shops. They include televisions, watches and motorcycles—to mention just a few.

Another industry in which Japan has made tremendous progress since the end of the Second World War is shipbuilding. Ships built in Japanese shipyards now sail on routes in all parts of the world and under flags of many nations. This is another industry which has helped to bring prosperity to a country which has little natural wealth.

While Japan's trade relations with countries throughout the world are now well established, she is still not on very friendly terms with some of her near neighbours.

The People's Republic of China is a Communist state which for many years was not recognized by the Japanese Government. This means that the two countries had no official dealings with each other. However, the Japanese Government changed its attitude in 1972, and since then relations with China have grown more friendly. With the Soviet Union—another near neighbour who was an enemy in the Second World War—Japan has not signed a peace treaty.

Japan has, however, tried to make good some of the damage done during the war. Some Asian countries reached agreement with Japan for sums of money to be paid to them in compensation for what they suffered.

Although the Japanese Constitution did not provide for an army for Japan, the country now has a Defence Force which is trained and equipped to meet any emergency which may arise. This Force was built up, with the help of the Allied Powers, at the time when all the American soldiers who had been in Japan since the end of the Second World War were moved to Korea where a new war broke out in 1950.

Although she now has a modern Defence Force, Japan is eager to encourage peace and international friendship throughout Asia and the rest of the world. She is a member of the United Nations Organization and is keen to co-operate in any effort to establish peace and prosperity. She participates in the regular economic summit meetings attended by the industrialized nations of the western world and plays a full part in international commerce and industry.

Index